WORLD MYTHOLOGY

MARS

by Jason Glaser

Consultant:
Dr. Laurel Bowman
Department of Greek and Roman Studies
University of Victoria
Victoria, British Columbia

Capstone
press

Mankato, Minnesota

Capstone Press
151 Good Counsel Drive, P.O. Box 669, Mankato, Minnesota 56002
www.capstonepress.com

Library of Congress Cataloging-in-Publication Data
Glaser, Jason.
    Mars / Jason Glaser; consultant, Laurel Bowman.
    p. cm.—(World mythology)
    Includes bibliographical references and index.
    ISBN 0-7368-2661-0 (hardcover)
    ISBN 0-7368-4714-6 (paperback)
    1. Mars (Roman deity)—Juvenile literature. [1. Mars (Roman deity). 2. Mythology,
Roman.] I. Title. II. Series: World mythology (Mankato, Minn.)
BL820.M2G57 2005
292.2′113—dc22   2003027203

Summary: An introduction to Mars and his role in Roman mythology, including his
connection with the Trojan War and such figures as Venus and Hercules.

Editorial Credits
Blake A. Hoena, editor; Juliette Peters, series designer; Patrick Dentinger, book designer
    and illustrator; Alta Schaffer and Wanda Winch, photo researchers; Eric Kudalis,
    product planning editor

Photo Credits
Art Resource, NY/Cameraphoto Arte, Venice, 20; Erich Lessing, 8; Réunion des Musées
    Nationaux, 4, 16; Scala, 18
Capstone Press/Gary Sundermeyer, cover (background), 1, 6
Corbis/Alexander Burkatowski, 14; Araldo de Luca, 10; NewSport/David Madison, 20 (top);
    Roger Wood, cover (statue)
DigitalVision, 20 (bottom)

1 2 3 4 5 6 09 08 07 06 05 04

TABLE OF CONTENTS

Ambroise Dubois painted this image of England's King Henry IV dressed as the war god Mars.

MARS

Mars was the Roman god of war. The Greeks called him Ares (AIR-eez). **Ancient** Greeks and Romans believed that Mars caused people to fight wars.

Ancient Greeks and Romans told many stories about Mars. In some stories, Mars fought in wars. During the **Trojan** War, he walked through the battlefield killing Greek soldiers.

In one battle, the goddess Minerva (mih-NUR-vuh) helped the Greek hero Diomedes (dye-uh-MEE-deez) attack Mars. Diomedes threw his spear at Mars. Minerva caused the spear to hit Mars in the chest.

Mars saw that Minerva had helped Diomedes. So Mars attacked her. He ran across the battlefield with his sword raised. Minerva picked up a rock and threw it at Mars. The rock knocked Mars to the ground. But he got up and continued to fight. Mars loved to fight. He could fight forever.

GREEK and ROMAN *Mythical Figures*

Greek Name: **APHRODITE**
Roman Name: **VENUS**
Goddess of love and beauty

Greek Name: **ATHENA**
Roman Name: **MINERVA**
Goddess of wisdom

Greek Name: **EROS**
Roman Name: **CUPID**
Mars' son and god of love

Greek Name: **HELIOS**
Roman Name: **SOL**
God of the sun

Greek Name: **HERA**
Roman Name: **JUNO**
Mars' mother and goddess of
marriage and childbirth

Greek Name: **HERACLES**
Roman Name: **HERCULES**
Greek hero who was Jupiter's son
and a rival of Mars

Greek Name: **HEPHAESTUS**
Roman Name: **VULCAN**
God of fire

Greek Name: **POSEIDON**
Roman Name: **NEPTUNE**
God of the sea

Greek Name: **PROMETHEUS**
Roman Name: **PROMETHEUS**
Titan who gave fire to humans

Greek Name: **ZEUS**
Roman Name: **JUPITER**
Ruler of the gods

Stories about gods such as Mars are called myths. Ancient Greeks and Romans told myths to explain many things. Some myths explained the cause of wars. Other myths told about gods, heroes, and monsters.

The god of war was not as important to the Greeks as he was to the Romans. The Greeks believed Ares made people angry and started fights. They felt Ares was a bully. Few Greeks liked him. Instead, they worshipped Athena (uh-THEE-nuh). Athena was the Greek name for Minerva. She fought to keep order and bring peace. Athena was also wise. The Greeks thought **wisdom** was important.

The Romans were more warlike than the Greeks. The Romans had strong armies and attacked many countries. To them, the god of war was one of the most important gods. Romans believed Mars protected Rome. They also believed Mars marched into battle in front of their armies.

The painting *Juno Sheds her Favors to Carthage*, by Eustache Le Sueur, shows Mars' mother, Juno.

Jupiter was the ruler of the gods. He swallowed his first wife, Metis (MEH-tuhss), while she was pregnant. Metis did not die. She was immortal. Jupiter only trapped her inside his body. He wanted to keep Metis from getting pregnant again.

One day, Jupiter had a bad headache. Jupiter asked the Titan Prometheus (proh-MEE-thee-uhss) to split his head open with an ax. Then they could see what was causing the headache. When Prometheus did as he was asked, Minerva leaped out of Jupiter's head. Minerva was Jupiter and Metis' daughter.

Jupiter was married to the goddess Juno when Minerva was born. Juno was angry that Jupiter had a child without her. She wanted to have a child without him. So Juno asked the goddess Flora to bring her a magical flower. The flower made Juno pregnant with Mars.

Juno's anger toward Jupiter was passed onto Mars. Mars was always angry. Most other gods stayed away from him.

In this ancient Roman sculpture, Mars (right) is shown with Venus (left) and his son Cupid (center).

MARS AND VENUS

Venus was the goddess of love and beauty. She loved Mars. Venus and Mars often spent time together. But they had to keep their love a secret. Venus was married to the god Vulcan.

Mars asked a boy named Alectryon (uh-LEK-tree-on) to help him. Alectryon made a noise to warn Mars whenever anyone might see him with Venus. But one night, Alectryon fell asleep. In the morning, the sun god Sol saw Mars and Venus together. Sol told the other gods about Mars and Venus.

Mars was angry with Alectryon. Mars turned Alectryon into a rooster. As a rooster, Alectryon crowed whenever he saw the sunrise. Ancient Greeks and Romans told this myth to explain why roosters crow at the sun in the morning.

Mars and Venus had many children together. Two of their children were warriors named Panic and Fear. Their son Cupid was the god of love.

In *The Judgement of Paris* by Sandro Botticelli, Paris (right) holds Discord's golden apple. Juno (left), Minerva (center left), and Venus (center right) wait for Paris to decide who gets the apple.

DISCORD'S TRICK

Mars had a sister named Discord. She liked to cause trouble and play tricks on the other gods. Discord once threw a gold apple at the feet of Juno, Minerva, and Venus. Discord said the apple belonged to the goddess who was the most beautiful. Juno, Minerva, and Venus argued over the apple. Each goddess thought she should get the apple.

Jupiter asked a Trojan prince named Paris to settle the argument between the goddesses. Each goddess offered Paris a gift if he gave her the apple. Venus' gift was Helen, the most beautiful woman in the world. Paris gave the apple to Venus.

Helen was already married to the king of Sparta, Greece. His name was Menelaus (meh-nuh-LAY-uhss). The Trojan War began when he led a Greek army to Troy to take Helen back from Paris.

Many gods were involved in the war. Juno and Minerva helped the Greek army. Venus helped Paris and the Trojans. Because Mars loved Venus, he also helped the Trojans.

Charles de Lafosse painted *Romulus and Remus*. Myths say that these twin sons of Mars were raised by a wolf.

During the Trojan War, Mars made the Trojan army very strong. Mars had his sons Panic and Fear and his nephew Strife make the Trojan soldiers fight hard. Mars also fought beside Hector, one of the Trojan leaders.

Juno asked Jupiter to force Mars away from the battle. Jupiter then sent Minerva to fight Mars. Minerva was a skilled fighter and never lost a battle. While Mars was busy fighting Minerva, the Greeks defeated the Trojans. They burned the city of Troy to the ground.

Venus helped Trojan Prince Aeneas (ih-NEE-uhss) escape from Troy. Venus was Aeneas' mother. Aeneas sailed from Troy to Italy. There, he founded the city of Alba Longa.

Rhea Silvia (REE-uh SILL-vee-uh) was one of Aeneas' **descendants**. Rhea Silvia and Mars had twin sons named Romulus (ROM-yoo-luhss) and Remus (REE-muhss). Myths said that Romulus founded the city of Rome.

Hercules (center left) battles Cycnus (center right) on this ancient Greek vase. Greeks decorated everyday items like vases, cups, and bowls with scenes from myths.

Jupiter's son Hercules was the strongest person on earth. Hercules and Mars often argued and fought. They were **rivals**.

Hercules killed several of Mars' children. Mars was the father of female warriors called Amazons. The Amazons' leader was Hippolyta (hih-PAW-luh-tuh). Mars gave Hippolyta a golden belt. One day, Hercules visited the Amazons in search of the belt. He killed Hippolyta to get the belt.

Mars' son Cycnus (SIK-nuhss) started a fight with Hercules. Hercules easily killed Cycnus. Angered by his son's death, Mars attacked Hercules. Jupiter stopped the fight, but Mars promised to get **revenge**.

Mars attacked Hercules many times. But Hercules was a skilled fighter and as strong as Mars. In one fight, Hercules beat Mars so badly that Mars could not get home. Mars' sons Panic and Fear had to carry him to Mount Olympus in Greece. In myths, Mount Olympus was the home of the gods.

18

Paolo Veronese painted *Mars and Neptune*. Mars is on the left, and Neptune is to the right.

Neptune was the god of the sea. He had a son named Halirrhothius (hal-ir-ROH-thee-uhss). Halirrhothius loved Mars' daughter Alcippe (al-SIH-pee). When Halirrhothius tried to catch Alcippe, Mars killed him.

Neptune thought Mars should be punished for his actions. But he was not strong enough to punish Mars alone. So Neptune called the other gods together. He asked them to punish Mars for killing his son.

The gods met on a hill to hold a **trial**. Myths said that this meeting was the first murder trial. Neptune argued why Mars should be punished. Mars argued that he had a good reason to kill Halirrhothius. Mars said he was protecting Alcippe. The gods agreed with Mars and did not punish him.

The hill where the gods met was named Areopagus. Areopagus means "hill of Ares." People from the Greek city of Athens once held all murder trials on this hill.

People compete in martial arts, such as Tae Kwon Do (above). Mars (right) is the fourth planet from the sun.

20

Ancient Greeks and Romans named many things after gods. The Romans called all ways of fighting martial arts after Mars. Modern types of martial arts include karate and Tae Kwon Do.

The Romans considered Mars a god of agriculture as well as a god of war. They named the month of March after Mars because they planted their crops in March. Romans also prepared to go to war in March.

Many objects in our solar system have Greek and Roman names. The fourth planet from the sun is called Mars. The Greeks called it Ares because they thought it looked blood red. The planet Mars has two moons, which are named Phobos and Deimos. These names are the Greek names for Mars' sons Panic and Fear.

People no longer believe that Greek and Roman myths are true. People now study myths. Myths help show what people believed a long time ago. Myths also entertain people. They are exciting stories about gods, heroes, and monsters.

Adriatic Sea

•Rome
•Alba Longa
ITALY

N
W • E
S

GREECE

•Troy

Aegean Sea

Thebes

Athens

Ionian Sea

Sparta

SICILY

LEGEND

• City

🏔 Mount Olympus

SCALE
Miles

| 0 | 100 | 200 |

| 0 | 100 | 200 |

Kilometers

CRETE

Mediterranean Sea

GLOSSARY

ancient (AYN-shunt)—having lived a long time ago

descendants (dih-SEND-unhtss)—a person's children and family members born after those children

immortal (i-MOR-tuhl)—able to live forever; ancient Greeks and Romans believed the gods were immortal.

revenge (rih-VENJ)—an action taken to cause harm to someone who has caused harm to you or someone you care about

rival (RYE-vuhl)—someone whom a person competes against

Titan (TYE-ten)—any one of the giants who ruled the world before the gods on Mount Olympus

trial (TRYE-uhl)—the act of finding out if someone is guilty or not guilty in a criminal case; Mars was put on trial for killing Neptune's son.

Trojan (TROH-juhn)—a person from the ancient city of Troy, or having to do with the city of Troy, such as the Trojan War

wisdom (WIZ-duhm)—knowledge and good judgement

READ MORE

Hoena, B. A. *Venus.* World Mythology. Mankato, Minn.: Capstone Press, 2003.

Nardo, Don. *Roman Mythology*. History of the World. San Diego: Kidhaven Press, 2002.

USEFUL ADDRESSES

National Junior Classical League
422 Wells Mill Drive
Miami University
Oxford, OH 45056

Ontario Classical Association
PO Box 19505
55 Bloor Street West
Toronto, ON M4W 3T9
Canada

INTERNET SITES

FactHound offers a safe, fun way to find Internet sites related to this book. All of the sites on FactHound have been researched by our staff.

Here's how:
1. Visit *www.facthound.com*
2. Type in this special code **0736826610** for age-appropriate sites. Or enter a search word related to this book for a more general search.
3. Click on the **Fetch It** button.

FactHound will fetch the best sites for you!

INDEX